J.J. FARR

For
Llewellyn Rees
to mark thirty-five years of friendship

RONALD HARWOOD

J.J. FARR

AMBER LANE PRESS

All rights whatsoever in this play are strictly reserved and
application for performance, etc. should be made before
rehearsal to:
Judy Daish Associates Ltd.
83 Eastbourne Mews
London W2 6LQ
No performance may be given unless a licence has been
obtained.

First published in 1988 by
Amber Lane Press Ltd.
9 Middle Way
Oxford OX2 7LH

Typeset in Ehrhardt by Oxford Computer Typesetting
Printed and manufactured in Great Britain by
Cotswold Press Ltd., Eynsham, Oxford

J.J. Farr by Ronald Harwood
suggested by the screenplay *Le Défroqué* (1952)
by Leo Joannon

Copyright © Paracier Holdings Ltd, 1988

ISBN: 0 906399 88 2

Other books by Ronald Harwood

Novels:
All the Same Shadows
The Guilt Merchants
The Girl in Melanie Klein
Articles of Faith
The Genoa Ferry
Cesar and Augusta

Short Stories:
One. Interior. Day. *Adventures in the Film Trade*

Biography:
Sir Donald Wolfit CBE: *His life and work in the unfashionable theatre**

Plays:
A Family
The Ordeal of Gilbert Pinfold (from Evelyn Waugh)*
The Dresser*
After the Lions*
Tramway Road*
The Deliberate Death of a Polish Priest*
Interpreters*

Miscellaneous:
A Night at the Theatre (Editor)
The Ages of Gielgud (Editor)
All the World's a Stage
Mandela

* *Published by Amber Lane Press*

J. J. Farr was first presented by Robert Fox and Memorial Films at the Theatre Royal, Bath, on Tuesday, 27 October 1987, and subsequently at The Phoenix Theatre, London, on 18 November 1987 with the following cast:

OLIVER BUDE	Dudley Sutton
KENNETH LOWRIE	Bob Peck
DENNIS MULLEY	Bernard Lloyd
ANDY ANDERSON	Trevor Peacock
AUSTIN PURVIS	Hugh Paddick
J.J. FARR	Albert Finney

Directed by Ronald Eyre
Designed by Jocelyn Herbert
Lighting by Rick Fisher

CHARACTERS

OLIVER BUDE
KENNETH LOWRIE
DENNIS MULLEY
ANDY ANDERSON
AUSTIN PURVIS
J.J. FARR

SET

A house in the country
A courtyard
J.J. Farr's temporary bedroom

The courtyard is formed by one corner of the house and is dominated
by a tree giving shade. Under the tree, a table and an assortment of
folding chairs. At more than one place steps lead down from a terrace
which borders the house on two sides. On each of these sides there are
French windows: one leads to the house; the other to J.J. Farr's
temporary bedroom which is austere and cell-like with a single bed, a
table and chair, a mirror on a chest of drawers. There are two doors in
this room: one to the bathroom and one to the house.

Summer

ACT ONE

SCENE ONE: Morning. Just after 9 a.m.

In J.J. FARR's *room,* DENNIS MULLEY *is making the bed.*

In the courtyard, OLIVER BUDE, *early 50s, an innocent, stands on a chair, fixing bunting to a tree.*

KENNETH LOWRIE, *45-ish, intense, highly-strung, comes out of the house.*

LOWRIE: Is this a good idea?

OLIVER: It has the Warden's blessing.

LOWRIE: What's your name again?

OLIVER: Oliver. Oliver Bude. I answer to anything except Olly.

LOWRIE: Is it a good idea to turn this into a festive occasion?

OLIVER: But it is a festive occasion, Mr Lowrie. The release of the hostages is cause for celebration.

LOWRIE: Where's the Warden?

OLIVER: Making the old waiting-room into temporary quarters for J.J. No stairs, you see. It has its own bathroom. And if the weather holds he can sit out here and recuperate. Do you really think the bunting's a mistake?

> [LOWRIE *paces restlessly.*]

LOWRIE: Is there anything I can do to help?

OLIVER: You could stop pacing. I'm quite jumpy enough as it is.

LOWRIE: Yes, well, I can't help it. I'm nervous of meeting him. He's been an important figure in my life — I wish it could be under more favourable circumstances —

> [DENNIS *comes out of* J.J. FARR's *room, stuffing a pillow into a pillow-slip. His age is difficult to guess, mid-60s, perhaps older. When he smiles it signals either self-mockery or secret amusement.*]

DENNIS: Any good at flowers, Mr Lowrie?

LOWRIE: Flowers?

DENNIS: The coloured things that grow in fields and gardens.

OLIVER: No, no, Warden, Austin does the flowers.

LOWRIE: Warden, I'm not sure about the bunting.

[LOWRIE *turns abruptly and goes back into the house.*]

OLIVER: Mr Lowrie makes me horribly nervous, Warden. He excretes disapproval. I do hope we haven't made a mistake admitting him.

DENNIS: J. J. will calm him down.

OLIVER: I seem to incur his displeasure. He never remembers my name. He reminds me of that dreadful Canadian, Monsignor Hepworth. Whenever he asked for my name, I thought, oh dear, I'm on his list. Another forty-seven thousand years in purgatory.

DENNIS: We must be gentle with Mr Lowrie. He had a particularly difficult time. I haven't really been able to welcome him properly, explain the ins and outs, our little peculiarities —
[*He smiles.*]

OLIVER: How's the room looking?

DENNIS: It needs flowers.

OLIVER: Austin'd be frightfully miffed if anybody else were to do the flowers.

DENNIS: Where is he?

OLIVER: Watching the television. He's been watching since seven o'clock this morning. How a man of his refinement can watch television and eat breakfast at the same time is one of the mysteries of the present century.
[ANDY ANDERSON, *50-ish, sad, haunted, always neatly dressed in shabby black, enters. He carries a sandwich tin.*]

ANDY: [*slightly frantic*] Is he here yet?

DENNIS: Not yet.

ANDY: Any idea when?

DENNIS: Soon.

ANDY: I won't sleep. I'll walk. I'll sleep later. I'll keep awake.
[*He is about to go when* AUSTIN PURVIS, *an exquisite old man, enters, carrying a canvas bag.*]

AUSTIN: I've seen J.J.

ANDY: Is he here?

AUSTIN: No, no, on the television —

DENNIS: You saw J.J.?

AUSTIN: Three times. They show it over and over again.

OLIVER: Why didn't you come out and call us?

AUSTIN: If I'd come out and called you, I'd have missed it.

DENNIS: How did he look?

AUSTIN: [*after consideration*] Not well. In fact, dreadful.

OLIVER: After five months in captivity you'd look dreadful, too.

DENNIS: Did he make a statement?

AUSTIN: No. We saw the aeroplane land. He and the other hostages were taken off but the camera was too far away to see clearly. Ants scurrying, nothing more. They were then escorted through the airport building into a large room where what I believe are called the media were gathered. A Foreign Office man, weedy, adenoidal, said that, under the circumstances, he was sure the media would understand if the released hostages declined to answer questions. But that was wishful thinking on his part because immediately the media started shouting questions with an insensitivity worthy of the Spanish Inquisition. The hostages were hurried out and that's when I saw J.J. He passed close to camera and looked straight at one. A bleak, demented look.

> [*Silence.*]

ANDY: I'm going to walk. I'll walk up the lane. I'll watch out for him. I've got to stay awake.

> [*He goes.*]

OLIVER: Perhaps Mr Lowrie's right. Perhaps the bunting is inappropriate.

DENNIS: Leave it. We want J.J. to feel he's welcome home.

> [AUSTIN *sits, takes embroidery from the canvas bag and begins to work at it.* DENNIS *goes back into* J.J.*'s room and continues with the bed-making.*]

AUSTIN: Television is absurd.

OLIVER: Then why watch it?

AUSTIN: They showed the same pictures of the hostages arriving three times within the hour. On the first occasion, just after 7 a.m. they flashed the word 'Live' on the screen. 'Live'. On the two subsequent showings, they flashed the word 'Recording'. Now, here's the absurdity: it is, in my view, impossible to verify that the first showing *was* live. How would one prove that it was not also a recording? The word 'live' in itself is proof of nothing except, in certain circumstances, the television company's intent to deceive. Even if one stood at the airport watching the aeroplane land while, at the same time, watching a television set showing the pictures of the landing, the one would not, in my view, be verification of the other. I must put that to J.J. That's very much his cup of tea.

OLIVER: I wish they'd make up their minds about J.J. When he was first taken hostage they called him, 'a former Catholic priest'—

AUSTIN: Which is accurate enough —

OLIVER: But during the captivity, when they found out more about him, he became, 'the well-known militant atheist'.

AUSTIN: Interesting. This morning, they described him as 'the distinguished Moral Philosopher'.

OLIVER: That's only since he was released. And I do find that a terrible affectation. One would never dream of describing anyone as an Immoral Philosopher.

AUSTIN: Yes, one would. Nietzsche.

OLIVER: Our Mr Lowrie watches us, you know. He stares as if trying to see through one. I'd look back at him but I'm frightened of being turned into a pillar of salt. [*mischievously*] I wonder how long it will be before he manages to tell J.J. that he's published a book.

AUSTIN: Under a minute.

> [OLIVER *finishes the bunting and climbs down off the chair.*]

OLIVER: You mustn't fuss J.J. with your little games, Austin, the moment he arrives.

AUSTIN: I know how to behave, thank you.

> [DENNIS *comes out of* J.J.'*s room carrying a vase.*]

DENNIS: Austin, be so kind as to arrange some flowers in this vase for J.J.'s room.

AUSTIN: [*fussed*] Will there be time? He should be here any moment.

> [LOWRIE *enters urgently.*]

LOWRIE: Warden, do we want a nurse?

DENNIS: What are you talking about?

LOWRIE: The telephone was ringing in the hall so I answered it. A Foreign Office official — difficult to understand, very nasal — speaking from the airport, wants to know if we need a nurse for Mr Farr or can we manage ourselves? Apparently he's not at all well. The Foreign Office bloke says he's a complete wreck, but they forgot about a nurse, and Mr Farr's on his way —

OLIVER: We don't need a nurse. Andy can cope —

DENNIS: Is he still on the telephone?

LOWRIE: Yes —

OLIVER: Warden, tell them we don't need a nurse.

[DENNIS *goes into the house, followed by* LOWRIE.]

LOWRIE: [*as he goes*] He should be here any second, he said.

OLIVER: I hope Dennis is firm with them. Andy is very capable. Unless there's blood, of course. He's had so much experience of hospitals, poor man. And, anyway, it would be quite unpractical. Where would we put a nurse? If it were a female she and J.J. would have to share a room and that would never do.

AUSTIN: Oh, don't be such a prude, Oliver. We're talking about a member of the medical profession.

OLIVER: Let me remind you that the medical profession is not above having unsavoury habits just like the rest of us. I trust you have not forgotten my little contretemps —

AUSTIN: Imagination —

OLIVER: It was not imagination. Dr Tomelty interfered with me.

AUSTIN: You were examined intimately, nothing more.

OLIVER: Allow me to be the judge of that.

AUSTIN: Certainly not. You're the least capable person of judging such things. You're a natural celibate. You've always said that celibacy was the least of your problems.

OLIVER: That doesn't alter the fact that Dr Tomelty told me to drop my trousers and the moment my back was turned she interfered with me.

[LOWRIE *enters, carrying a couple of books.*]

LOWRIE: Do you think Mr Farr will mind if I ask him to sign a couple of his books?

OLIVER: Not the moment he arrives.

LOWRIE: No, no, no. I'll just put them down — the opportunity may — they're both a bit battered —

AUSTIN: So I see.

LOWRIE: I've read them. Countless times. All his works, really. I know whole passages — they've meant a lot to me. There are books that mean — a lot.

AUSTIN: Which particular ones do you want him to inscribe?

LOWRIE: *Seeing, Not Believing* and *After God.*

OLIVER: I never got through *Seeing, Not Believing.* Much too intellectual for me. But even I managed to read *After God.*

AUSTIN: Yes, you would. The doubting man's guide to certainty. Such a vulgar little work. The title page summed it all up. *After God. J.J. Farr.*

OLIVER: It did a lot to popularise his thought.

AUSTIN: Precisely. And do you remember, Oliver, all those cheap little jokes so beloved of those cheap little reviewers? Not Farr enough. Farr too Farr. Farr Off. Farr Out. We did tease him.

OLIVER: Farr Better. Farr Worse.

AUSTIN: He doesn't like being teased.

LOWRIE: Is he very forbidding?

AUSTIN: Distant. Not forbidding.

OLIVER: Can be fierce. He sometimes looks at people as though he's come to arrest them.

AUSTIN: Boyish. He reminds me of a lad who was at school with me. Brainbox, we called him. J.J.'s like that. A clever little boy who can explain away fear of the dark.

OLIVER: Andy's the only one who can make him laugh. He tells J.J. dirty jokes and sings him obscene ditties. Odd, isn't it?

LOWRIE: *Seeing, Not Believing* — at the time of my — my crisis — contorted my mind.

OLIVER: [*with genuine concern*] Was that a good thing?

AUSTIN: I used to be able to do the opening sentence. 'In the dying years of the present century, no reasonable person can be reasonable and religious.' I've always thought those words very striking.

LOWRIE: That's in the *Oxford Book of Quotations* now, you know.

AUSTIN: Well, yes, I remember it all caused quite a stir at the time.

OLIVER: Did it not. Cardinal Bingham described J.J. as the devil incarnate.

AUSTIN: But then Cardinal Bingham was always given to understatement.

OLIVER: What's the opening sentence of your book, Mr Lowrie? I do think opening sentences are frightfully important, don't you? I like all books to begin, 'A shot rang out!' How does your book begin?

LOWRIE: 'Faith in the supernatural is a neurotic device to deaden fear of death.'

AUSTIN: You and J.J. should get on well.

LOWRIE: I tell you this: if he is a complete wreck it'll be physical not mental. Farr has the sort of intellect that's not easily intimidated. There was one report that struck me as particularly telling. The go-between, that obscene little lawyer, Dr Fawzi, when asked by a reporter how J.J. Farr was bearing up, said, remarkably well, except that he was extremely unpopular with his fellow Christians. I thought to myself, I bet he is. And when Fawzi said in that smug, cigarette-choked voice, 'God is not mocked, you know', I thought, he is by J.J. Farr.

[*He laughs.* ANDY *rushes in.*]

ANDY: He's here, he's here, J.J.'s here, he's coming round the side, I'm going to fetch him —

OLIVER: How does he look?

ANDY: Get Dennis —

[ANDY *exits hurriedly.*]

OLIVER: Where is he?

LOWRIE: On the telephone —

AUSTIN: [*overlapping*] Somewhere in the house.

[J.J. FARR *enters, helped by* ANDY, *who carries,* J.J.'s *suitcase.*]

[J.J. *could be anything from mid-40s to mid-50s. He is pale, drawn. He is wearing clothes that are obviously brand new, a hat, but no jacket. He walks with difficulty. His struggle to appear in control is immense. Awkward silence.*]

OLIVER: Welcome home, J.J.

J.J.: I thought of you all often.

AUSTIN: Dear J.J.

J.J.: I'm rather tired.

OLIVER: Oughtn't you to sit?

LOWRIE: Would someone introduce us?

OLIVER: Yes, of course. J.J., this is a new resident, Kenneth Lowrie.

[LOWRIE *offers a hand but* J.J. *doesn't respond.*]

J.J.: Have we met before?

LOWRIE: No, but you did once review a book of mine in the TLS. Favourable. *The Externalization of Demons.*

J.J.: I don't remember.

AUSTIN: [*quietly to* OLIVER] And such a catchy title.

[OLIVER *suppresses a nervous giggle, like a child, hand covering the mouth.*]

ANDY: I have to sleep now. Pleased to see you, J.J. We thought about you an awful lot, too. A minute of silent thought every morning for the whole five months. Oliver's idea.

J.J.: Where's Dennis Mulley?

OLIVER: He'll be here presently —

J.J.: And David Ingham? Why have we got a new resident? What's happened to David?

OLIVER: David was taken ill some weeks ago. He collapsed suddenly here in the garden. He went very peacefully and quietly. He didn't suffer.

[J.J. *removes his hat and crosses himself.*]

ANDY: [*alarmed and astonished*] J.J. —

[*They all watch* J.J., *amazed. His eyes are closed and his lips move. Then he opens his eyes.*]

J.J.: I ought to warn you of something. I don't know what you've been told but it's best you hear the facts from me. I was examined in Cyprus by doctors. They came to the conclusion that I'm mentally deranged —

[*He tries to laugh but is dangerously near tears.*]

OLIVER: Now, now, J.J., oughtn't you to go straight to bed?

J.J.: You mustn't treat me like a naughty boy. Which I am — [*He forces a smile.*] Here's the problem. My memory, at the moment, is selective. I recall some events with burning clarity. Other things — It's a mild form of hysteria, a blocking out. Understandable. In the circumstances. That's what's so fascinating to me. I can see myself but the self I see is blind. I'm rational and irrational. I seem to be suffering — according to these doctors — from some sort of reversion — I've reverted — [*He stops himself.*] — that's not quite right — well, well, all in good time — I can, like now, talk about myself as if I were someone else. But when I am that someone else I can't talk at all. It's the crying that deceived the medical men — I'm going to cry at any moment now — the doctors take it to be a sign of mental and emotional instability. But it's the residual pain of an unwanted experience, the pleasure of a joyous struggle, and the certainty of a glorious victory in which I want you all to share —

[*He fights tears.* DENNIS *enters.*]

DENNIS: J.J. Welcome home. Welcome home. Let me look at you. You're pale. I thought you'd have a splendid suntan. Any-

way, you look ten years younger than when I last saw you.
Come, let's be un-English and embrace.

> [DENNIS *hugs* J.J., *who screams out in pain, almost faints.
> He whimpers pitifully.* ANDY *dashes to hold him.*]

ANDY: Better get him to his room —

> [ANDY *escorts* J.J. *to his room and helps him on to the bed.*]

J.J.: [*in terror*] Don't touch my back — not my back —

> [J.J. *lies face down on the bed.*]

ANDY: [*shying away*] You're bleeding.

J.J.: [*barely audible*] *Domine, non sum dignus* —

ANDY: What's wrong with your back? Should I get Dr Tomelty?

J.J.: They punished me — pills — pills in the bag.

> [ANDY *finds the pills, and goes into the bathroom.* J.J.
> *cries.* ANDY *returns with a glass of water and helps* J.J. *to
> take the pills.*]

> [*During this,* DENNIS *turns, ill at ease, to the others.*]

DENNIS: You make an effort to be welcoming and that's the thanks
you get.

> [*He smiles. Silence.*]

OLIVER: He's dreadfully ill.

DENNIS: Apparently.

OLIVER: But you didn't see what we saw. He crossed himself and
prayed.

> [DENNIS *tries to smile.*]

He asked after David and when I told him that David had
died —

> [*Silence.*]

AUSTIN: I was much more perturbed by his language. 'A joyous
struggle, a glorious victory' does not bode well. He seems
broken.

> [*Silence.* ANDY *comes back into the courtyard.*]

ANDY: He's got some sort of wound on his back. He says they
punished him. Better get Dr Tomelty. She'll clean it, dress
it. I've given him a sedative. Valium-based. Think he'll
sleep.

AUSTIN: I shall pick flowers for his room.

J.J.: [*crying out*] Charlatan! *Hic est, hoc est!* Open the cage! Open
the cage! Hey presto, we have blood! Wants a priest — he
wants a priest! *Ce n'est pas nécessaire, il est mort* —

ANDY: Never thought to hear night-noises at this time of the
          morning.
                    [ANDY *goes back into the room and watches over him.*]
J.J.:   [*moaning again*] Allahu Akbar, Allahu Akbar. Pater noster, qui
          es in coelis, sanctifecetur nomen tuum. Adveniat regnum tuum.
          Fiat voluntas tua —
                    [*His words become mumbled; the mumbling turns into
                    moaning.*]
LOWRIE: Crossing himself, J.J. Farr, incredible.
DENNIS: You obviously have a gift, Mr Lowrie, for the economical
          turn of phrase.
                    [*He goes.*]
                    [*Silence.*]
                    [*Lights fade to blackout.*]

SCENE TWO: *Noon. Eight days later.*

In his room, J.J. *is putting on his shirt with great care. There is a
dressing covering a wound in the small of his back. When he
finishes, he exits into the bathroom.*

LOWRIE, *seated at the table under the tree, is writing furiously,
referring to two or three books.* ANDY *sleeps in the shade.*

DENNIS *enters.*

DENNIS: Mr Lowrie, would you mind, now?
                    [LOWRIE *begins to gather up his papers.*]
LOWRIE: And how's the hostage getting on?
DENNIS: Slowly.
LOWRIE: Still praying, is he?
                    [*No response.*]
          I want to ask you something, Warden. I'll be blunt.
DENNIS: When are you anything else?
LOWRIE: Are you equipped to deal with him?
                    [*No response.*]
          You let him talk to you. He's been talking every day for over
          a week. Is your conversation structured in any way? Do you
          know about the trigger words? He shouts at night. He keeps
          me awake. I've been making notes of what he says. They may

be helpful. Put them to him, take him off guard, surprise
him, shock him. Do you know anything about confrontation
techniques?

[*No response.*]

You just let him ramble on, do you? I mean, what's the
burden of your conversation?

[*Pause.*]

DENNIS: I was once, years ago, for a short while, his confessor.

LOWRIE: [*backing off*] All right, all right, all right. Because I've done
some work in this area —

DENNIS: Have you?

LOWRIE: You've not read my book?

DENNIS: No.

LOWRIE: I deal in some detail with the relationship between psychosis
and religion.

DENNIS: Sounds fascinating.

LOWRIE: I have a chapter on Farr's sort of strategy. It's a hysteric
manoeuvre. A touch of aggression can be remarkably effec-
tive therapy. I don't suppose you'd let me have a go at him?

DENNIS: No.

LOWRIE: Patients find it difficult to maintain the psychotic-religious
mode when attacked. It's in my book.

DENNIS: When I have time I must give it a whirl.

LOWRIE: [*exploding*] Stop disparaging me, I'm not someone to be
disparaged.

DENNIS: I never disparage anyone except myself —

LOWRIE: I'm not one of your relics, Warden. My disgrace wasn't
closet queenery or altar boys or piss artistry. My struggle was
intellectual —

DENNIS: Calmly, Mr Lowrie, I didn't mean to upset you —

LOWRIE: The only indecency of which I was guilty was trying to
expose an ancient, debilitating psychosis. Not an opiate. An
illness. My bishop told me this was a place 'to hang up my
collar' for a while, a place where one could contemplate, a
community which was meant to re-educate not embalm, a
place to recover, to take stock. I told him I'd prefer the
hostel in the Holloway Road, where there were *real* people.
No, he said, this was the place for me. And what do I find?
The air fetid with the smell of stale bread and sour wine. It
needs fumigating. You want to get rid of the male spinsters,

Warden, the crypto-or-not-so-crypto-homosexuals. The
world has changed —

DENNIS: I know you've had a bad time, Mr Lowrie, but I want to
assure you that —

LOWRIE: [*cutting in, almost continuous, embattled*] — Yes, yes, a bad
time, yes, because how do you make it clear that man has to
learn to love himself not God? Yes, I had a bad time trying to
bring reason to bear on a dead mythology, trying to make
others understand that the only paradise we'll ever know is
on this earth and of our making. We have to work, not pray.
You, me, all of them, should be out there working, doing
socially useful work. If they really want to know what hell's
like —

DENNIS: [*a smile*] I'm not sure they do —

LOWRIE: [*continuing*] — let them visit the inner cities, let them put
their energies into alleviating poverty in this world, now.
They're parasites, behaving as though they were still priests,
poncing off the community —

DENNIS: So are you, Mr Lowrie, so am I, still priests, I mean,
technically at least —

LOWRIE: No. Not me. Well, technically, perhaps, but in no other way.

DENNIS: [*a smile*] And I'm not sure I approve of the word 'poncing'.
We are beneficiaries of a Trust, set up a hundred years ago,
to provide a home where men like us may learn to ease the
pain of loss —

LOWRIE: You see? You see? Loss, the pain of loss. What loss? We're
free. We've broken our compulsions and doubts. We've lost
nothing. But you and the others still seem to cling involuntarily to your superstitions and tribal rites. I can't identify any
one thing, but I have the impression that you behave not like
ex-priests but failed priests. And if there are to be houses
like this, Trusts set up 'to ease the pain of loss', let them be
filled with men of real distinction who can point us in other
directions, help us to find a new heaven. On this earth. Now.
Philosophers, logicians, psychologists, sociologists. This
place could become a centre of excellence, instead of a
genteel geriatric clinic. Put the present bunch out to work,
Warden. They'll soon stop feeling the pain of loss.

DENNIS: And J.J. Farr?

LOWRIE: Ah, yes, former Father Farr. He shouldn't be here. He

needs proper treatment and I don't think you're equipped to
give it. I can let you have the name of someone —

DENNIS: Thank you, I appreciate it but let's see, shall we? No, don't
go. [*Pause.*] You may be able to help.

> [DENNIS *takes a letter from his pocket.*]

> [*In his room,* J.J. *returns. He goes down on all fours and
> rests his hands and head on the bed. From time to time he
> straightens and seems to sway.*]

You say you've heard him crying out at night —

LOWRIE: My notes, you're welcome to them —

DENNIS: Thank you. But — have you ever heard him mention the
name Magee?

LOWRIE: Magee?

DENNIS: A Jesuit. Father Liam Magee. It's important.

LOWRIE: No, I don't think so. Why?

DENNIS: [*scanning the letter*] This Father Magee was held in the same
place as the hostages, although not one of them. Apparently,
J.J. was with him when he died. The Irish Embassy want to
know what happened. And so, of course, does the priest's
mother. So, if he ever mentions the name Magee, in any
context, will you let me know?

> [DENNIS *goes to* J.J.*'s room but, seeing* J.J. *on his knees,
> returns to the courtyard. Meanwhile,* LOWRIE *has made a
> note of something.*]

He's — he's at prayer.

LOWRIE: And I used to think J.J. Farr peed eau-de-Cologne.

DENNIS: Well, perhaps now a more appropriate metaphor would be
holy water.

> [*He smiles.*]

LOWRIE: He shouldn't be here.

> [*He goes.* ANDY *rises.*]

ANDY: That man's in pain. Terrible pain.

DENNIS: You were awake, you ought to have made it known.

ANDY: Difficult to sleep with him banging about. Why are people
always so aggressive in the face of conviction? I wonder if he
was a convert. [*quietly, to* DENNIS] Dr Tomelty says J.J.'s
wound is still festering.

DENNIS: Did she say what happened?

ANDY: I forgot to ask her. I'm not at ease in her presence. She's so

awfully well-endowed. I wish there were something really
wrong with me, she could do me a terrible injury.

DENNIS: Go back to sleep, Andy. In your room.

ANDY: [*with an appropriate gesture*] She's — colossal. I mean, have
you ever seen such bazonkers?

DENNIS: Seldom.

> [*In his room* J.J. *finishes his prayers.*]

> [DENNIS *begins to arrange two chairs under the tree.*]

ANDY: There was a nurse in St. Augustine's. Molly, her name was.
She had big bazonkers, too. When she came to give me my
medicine, I'd pretend I couldn't sit up. She'd bend over me.
Then, as she said, 'Now, be a good boy,' I'd grab 'em. Oh,
what a fondle was there my countrymen. Joyous, truly
joyous. She fell for it every time, did Molly. She probably
enjoyed it. 'Now, be a good boy,' and all hands on breasts.
Joyous, joyous. 'And you a man of the cloth,' she'd say.

> [J.J. *comes out of his room.*]

[*to* J.J.] Talking about bazonkers, J.J.

> [J.J. *smiles faintly.*]

Now, be a good boy —

> [*He goes.*]

> [J.J. *nods to* DENNIS, *then sits. The chairs have been
> arranged in an odd way:* J.J.'s *chair is placed sideways on
> to the other. The effect of this will be that* J.J. *will look at*
> DENNIS *while he talks, but* DENNIS *will not look at* J.J.]

> [*A long silence.*]

J.J.: I'm still in the cage.

DENNIS: Literally a cage?

J.J.: Literally. Shouting abuse. What happened while I was in the
cage, on the eighteenth Sunday of our captivity, is, I know,
crucial. But I can't seem to — I can't — or won't — or don't
want to —

> [*He begins to pant in panic.*]

DENNIS: In your own time, J.J., in your own time —

J.J.: Why did I shout abuse, I'll get to it, I'll get to it, but why — ?

DENNIS: Don't force it. Let the wind blow, let the wind take the dry,
dead leaves.

> [*Silence.*]

J.J.: Did I tell you about the lecture?

DENNIS: No.

J.J.: I remembered last night. On the day we were taken, I'd given a lecture. The title was: 'Faith and logic: the continuing conflict'. The usual drivel. I talked for an hour without notes. Afterwards, the Professor who introduced me said that it was a dangerous subject 'in this day and age'. I went back to the hotel, showered, changed, and then heard a commotion in the corridor. I opened my door and that's when I came face to face with a gunman wearing a black hood. Have I told you that?

DENNIS: About the gunman, yes.

J.J.: Have I told you that twelve of us were kept in one hotel room for two days and nights in squalid conditions?

DENNIS: Yes, and that blindfold you were taken to a prison. But you didn't want to talk about the prison.

[*Silence.*]

J.J.: Old, foul-smelling, airless. Nine of us are put three to a cell. The remaining three men are given separate cells. That, we all know, is ominous because one's an American — a travel agent; the second, an Israeli television producer; the third, a Jew, a French economist. We are guarded by men and, I think, women, whose faces we never see. To keep our spirits up, one of my cell-mates, Jimmy Martin, a freelance journalist from Melbourne, sings.

[*Pause; he sings softly.*]

'O dear, what can the matter be?
Three old ladies locked in the lavatory,
They were there from Monday to Saturday,
Nobody knew they were there.'

[*Pause.*]

But that soon stopped. He was beaten. Our guards were high on hash or coke, which of course licensed their brutality.

[*He shudders.*]

[*with a puzzled look*] I remember something from my lecture. 'What are we to make of terror? Gangster ethics born of a single resentment. Revenge feeding revenge. Helplessness and rage. Continuous defeats and small victories. How are we to understand nihilism — the dive into nothing? How are we to understand it?'

DENNIS: I thought, from what I've seen and heard, that you might again have found the way.
[*Silence.*]
J.J.: On the third Sunday, a strange thing occurred. We were visited by a priest, Macnee or Magee, it was never clear. Our captors, being themselves believers, encouraged belief in their captives, which was oddly symmetrical.
DENNIS: [*smiles*] Can something be oddly symmetrical?
J.J.: Perhaps not, perhaps. This priest had been inside for over eighteen months, a prisoner of the old regime, but not freed in the general amnesty, forgotten, weak, ill, shivering with fever. There were six Papists among us including the American travel agent and my cell-mate, Jimmy Martin —
DENNIS: Do you count yourself in that number?
J.J.: Yes, Father Macnee or Magee heard their confessions through the iron bars of their cells, absolved them and gave them the Eucharist out of a tin or enamel mug, a stale crust on a battered plate. He recognised me. He said, 'I know you.' And I said, 'Leave me alone. I don't want anything to do with you.' He nodded sadly and passed on. Each Sunday thereafter he came to us but ignored me. Then, there were dreadful events. On successive days, the American, the Israeli and the French Jew were taken out and shot. When the priest next appeared I began shouting abuse at him, obscenities, as if blaming him for what had happened. I can't explain that yet.
DENNIS: Not everything can be explained.
J.J.: The more I tried to stop myself shouting, the more vehement I became.
DENNIS: What sort of things?
[J.J. *shakes his head, refusing to speak.*]
[*Silence.*]
[DENNIS *takes the letter from his pocket.*]
And this Father Magee died, did he?
J.J.: [*alarmed*] What?
DENNIS: They say you were with him when he died.
J.J.: Who says? Where did you get that from? What's that got to do with anything? Who says I was with him?
DENNIS: Easy, J.J., easy —

J.J.: Easy, easy, what are you talking about? Why do you ask about Macnee out of the blue, where do you get it from?

DENNIS: Some inquiry or other, his mother wants to know about his death —

J.J.: What about his death? Is she doubting my credentials, what's it about, I was there, it was all right — ?

DENNIS: Tell me, then —

J.J.: [*savage*] He died and they desecrated his body, that's all, easy, easy.

[*Silence.*]

[DENNIS *puts away the letter.*]

DENNIS: Tell me about the cage, the literal cage.

[*No response.*]

Is this the block?

[*No response.*]

Is this where memory selects? Is this the cage in which the memory is also imprisoned?

[*No response.*]

If the cage is literal, who put you there and why?

J.J.: [*suddenly*] Is the local man going to come and see me?

DENNIS: No.

J.J.: Why not?

DENNIS: His bishop has fobidden him to visit this house.

J.J.: That's criminal.

DENNIS: Bishops often are.

J.J.: How long have I been back?

DENNIS: Eight days. Eight days today.

J.J.: I want to go for a walk tomorrow —

DENNIS: Yes, fine —

[*Silence.*]

Why did they put you in the cage?

J.J.: [*slightly aggressive*] All right, I'll tell you, if you're so interested, of course I'll tell you, nothing very terrible, if you feel obliged to know —

DENNIS: Only if it's important —

J.J.: You be the judge of that, you tell me how important it is —

DENNIS: [*smiling*] The old ways, the old days.

J.J.: The Papists.

DENNIS: Yes?

J.J.: After the third execution, after the French Jew died, our captors stopped the priest visiting the cells.

DENNIS: Why?

J.J.: Difficult to say. The theory was that he'd been with the American when the American was executed and they didn't want us to learn the details, there was no rational explanation, there never is —

DENNIS: Why the cage?

J.J.: I'm getting there, I'm getting there.

DENNIS: [*smiling*] Dry, dead leaves.

> [LOWRIE's *face appears at a window, watching them, secretly.*]

J.J.: One of the Papists put in a request that we be allowed to attend Mass on Sunday. There were days of negotiation. In the end, on Sundays, we, the five remaining Papists, were led to a tunnel, dark and low. Jimmy Martin said, 'This leads to an arena and we're going to be eaten by lions.' But at the end of the tunnel we found ourselves in a cage. Like in a circus. An animal cage. Iron bars on wheels, used a long time ago to transport criminals from place to place. And, in this cage, we were wheeled into the prison yard.

DENNIS: The literal cage.

J.J.: Yes, yes, I said, I objected. I didn't want — I had no interest — but my complaints were disregarded. So. On Sundays we'd be wheeled into the prison yard and the priest would come in tattered, stained vestments, and those of us who wanted to attend were let out of the cage. On all but one occasion I remained behind the bars. Shouting my abuse.

DENNIS: During his Mass?

J.J.: Oh yes, during his Mass, of course, when else? Yes, yes, during his Mass, all right.

DENNIS: But he ignored you. [*smiles*] Or tried to.
> [*Silence.*]

J.J.: Someone complained.

DENNIS: The priest?

J.J.: No, no, not the priest, not the priest. I must go for a walk tomorrow —

DENNIS: Yes, yes. [*Pause.*] Who complained?

J.J.: I don't know. Never found out. But I was punished and told not to do it again.

DENNIS: Punished how?

J.J.: I was told God is not mocked. No. God is not mocked. Help me with my dressing —

DENNIS: No, J.J., not now — let Dr Tomelty —

J.J.: Yes, now. I want to show you —

> [*He takes off his shirt, an obviously painful task. He manages to remove the dressing.* LOWRIE *sees* J.J.*'s wound first, and recoils from the sight.* J.J. *turns to show* DENNIS. *On his back is a festering sore.*]

Can you see what it is?

DENNIS: [*very calm*] No.

J.J.: It's a cross.

DENNIS: Is it? I can't tell. Did they cut that into you?

J.J.: No. They branded me.

> [*He stands, showing* DENNIS *the wound on his back.*]
> [*Lights fade to blackout.*]

SCENE THREE: Two days later. 4 p.m.

J.J.*'s room is empty.*

LOWRIE *sets up a table and puts a tablecloth on.* OLIVER *and* ANDY *carry cushions on from the house.* AUSTIN *enters.* DENNIS *brings on a tray of food for the picnic.* LOWRIE *exits.*

OLIVER: [*when* LOWRIE *is out of the way*] He didn't really say we should have sociologists here, did he?

ANDY: Yes, and philosophers and logicians.

OLIVER: But sociologists. Can one think of anything more boring?

ANDY: Yes. Nuclear physicists, they're more boring. Very tiresome people, nuclear physicists.

AUSTIN: Her late Majesty the Queen of Portugal was a very tiresome person.

OLIVER: Oh, do concentrate, Austin. She's not likely to come here, is she? In the first place she's dead. In the second, we don't take old queens.

DENNIS: I'm not sure Mr Lowrie would agree.

> [ANDY *laughs intensely but stops just as* LOWRIE *enters from the house with a plastic bucket. They all become*

*faintly embarrassed. He puts down the bucket and goes
back into the house.*]

OLIVER: Of course, if he said he wants us to do useful work, that, you
may depend on it, was a dig at me. I make no secret of the
fact that I have capital. It'd be immoral for me to work. I'd be
taking a job from somebody who really needed one. But I
visit prisons. That's useful. At least, to the prisoners. One
hopes. And you, Dennis, nobody works harder than you.
Where would we all be without you? And Andy. It can't be
much fun being a nightwatchman. But it's useful. It's guard-
ing society against criminals.

ANDY: And fires. That's my chief worry. Fires.

[LOWRIE *returns with four or five ice trays, and proceeds
to empty the cubes into the plastic bucket.* DENNIS *helps
him.*]

LOWRIE: And will Mr Farr be joining us?

DENNIS: I hope so.

LOWRIE: He's going for walks now, isn't he? Twice a day. I followed
him.

DENNIS: I hope the exercise did you both good.

LOWRIE: You know where he goes, don't you?

[*No response.*]

The illness is easily identified. I call it in my book 'Waferitis'.

DENNIS: The *bon mot* as ever, Mr Lowrie. [*to* ANDY] Time to fetch
him.

[ANDY *goes round the side of the house.*]

When J.J. joins us, let's keep things jolly.

[LOWRIE *goes back into the house.*]

AUSTIN: My mother used to say that to me annually, each birthday,
just as the guests were about to arrive. 'Austin-dear,' she'd
say, 'you mustn't mind if the other children play with the
presents they bring you. We must keep things jolly.' It always
ended in tears, but never mine.

[ANDY *escorts* J.J. *into the courtyard. He seems more
rested.*]

J.J.: When I was in captivity, the heat was unbearable and I used
to daydream about the English weather, longing for grey
skies, and scattered showers. Instead I come back into a
heatwave. Typical.

DENNIS: Here's your chair, J.J. —

OLIVER: Don't you look well, J.J.?

ANDY: Dr Tomelty gives him his pills lying down, that's why —
[*Uneasy silence.*]

AUSTIN: Did I ever tell you my story about the pearls and the Queen of Portugal, J.J.?

OLIVER: Of course you did, dozens of times.
[*Pause.*]

AUSTIN: The Queen of Portugal was on a private visit to London. After attending Mass, she invited me to have breakfast with members of her household and some female friends. At Claridges. In her suite. I was the only male present and, therefore, seated on the Queen's right. Presently she turned to me and said, 'Isn't it terrible, Monsignor, how standards have declined? I've looked around this table,' she said, 'and I see only four gals wearing real pearls.' 'Forgive me, ma'am,' I replied — [*He unbuttons his shirt to show that he is wearing a string of pearls.*] — 'five.'
[LOWRIE *returns with three or four bottles of hock, which he puts in the plastic bucket.*]

DENNIS: The wine's on Oliver.
[*Murmurs of thanks.* LOWRIE *pulls the first cork to cheers.*]

ANDY: Festivities are about to commence.

OLIVER: And, Andy, don't drink too much. You know it makes you weep.

DENNIS: Tuck in. Mr Lowrie will do the wine. I'll do J.J.
[*They all help themselves.* DENNIS *brings a plate to* J.J.]

OLIVER: What fun this is. Isn't this fun?

ANDY: [*about to eat*] Benedic, Domine, nos et haec tua dona quae de tua largitate sumus sumpturi. Per Christum Dominum nostrum.
[*He crosses himself.* J.J. *puts a hand to his forehead as though beginning the Sign of the Cross, but lets it rest there. Then all, except* J.J., *begin to eat in silence.*]

J.J.: Did I tell you, Andy, we used to sing dirty songs in the prison? [*He hums the tune of 'Three Old Ladies'.*] But I've forgotten the words —

ANDY: [*singing*] 'Oh dear, what can the matter be?
Three old ladies locked in a lavatory —'
[J.J. *begins to cry silently.*]

DENNIS: All right, Andy, not now —

[ANDY *suddenly moves round to* J.J.]

ANDY: J.J., old chap, dear old chap, I don't know the details, but I can guess. I don't envy you. I wouldn't have survived as you've survived. A chap doesn't expect to travel the Damascus road twice in a lifetime. I can't remember what faith was like, it was so long ago. And I was always a fallen angel. I've only really thought about one thing all my life. And what's it matter? It may all soon be over at any moment for all of us. [*He looks skyward.*] Now. Now. What price *Pacem in terris*? No good watching for fires, then. The fire will be too big. It can happen at any moment. Now. Now. When that chap wrote 'the horror! the horror!' he was still sucking at his mother's nipples.

J.J.: It's unbearably hot, I'm burning —

OLIVER: Really, Andy, what's the point of giving you a party if you're going to be so depressing?

[J.J. *mops sweat from his face.*]

ANDY: Dear J.J., dear old chap, you seem to have walked through unwanted fire back into the sun. And that's an unenviable thing.

[*Silence.*]

OLIVER: [*almost a sigh*] Yes, yes, yes, yes, yes.

[DENNIS *starts a round of 'Happy Birthday.'*]

[*Silence.*]

[LOWRIE *watches* J.J. *and comes near to him, calculating, determined.*]

LOWRIE: There's something I've been longing to ask you, Mr Farr —

J.J.: Yes?

LOWRIE: It's about this change of mind or heart you seem to have suffered.

DENNIS: No, Mr Lowrie, not now, this is meant to be Andy's party.

LOWRIE: [*overlapping*] Is that what the doctors meant when they said — [*in the clear*] — you'd suffered a reversion?

J.J.: We are what we have always been.

AUSTIN: [*trying to lighten the atmosphere*] Oh, good. J.J., you must be on the mend. I've been waiting for one of your little aphorisms. I've always enjoyed your lecturettes on logic and rationality. They seemed to me quite as absurd as anything else. But there's a puzzle I want to put to you about television —

LOWRIE: Hold on a minute, what did you mean, Mr Farr? We are what we've always been?

DENNIS: Go on about television, Austin —

LOWRIE: No. I'd like to hear what Mr Farr has to say. That's a provocative statement, we are what we've always been. Did you mean that in a general sense, or were you being specific, about us?

J.J.: Specific. About you, about me, about all of us here.

LOWRIE: Then we're entitled to an explanation —

DENNIS: No, we're not, Mr Lowrie —

LOWRIE: Stop protecting him, Warden. Let's hear what he has to say. He's vocal enough at night, keeping us all awake —

DENNIS: Mr Lowrie, I forbid this —

LOWRIE: Why do you shout out, Mr Farr? Why do you talk in code?

J.J.: What d'you mean, code? I don't shout out —

LOWRIE: Oh yes, you do. The messages are in code but we don't have the key, only you have the key —

OLIVER: Isn't it time for J.J.'s rest?

LOWRIE: No, it isn't time for his rest, he's only just joined us —

OLIVER: Another time, then, another time —

LOWRIE: *Hic est*, abracadabra, we have blood, what's it about, Mr Farr?

J.J.: Where did you hear that?

LOWRIE: That's not wine, that's urine —

J.J.: Where do you hear these things?

LOWRIE: From you, crying out at night, crying out for help —

J.J.: When, when, when do I cry out?

ANDY: I don't hear you, J.J., I'm at work —

LOWRIE: We hear you, we hear you —

OLIVER: Yes, we hear him, but what's it matter, not now, please, not now —

LOWRIE: [*overlapping*] Wine, urine, blood, you keep us awake at night —

J.J.: I'm drugged, I don't know what I'm saying. I'm drugged —

LOWRIE: He wants a priest —

J.J.: What?

LOWRIE: Charlatan —

J.J.: I was in the cage —

LOWRIE: Open the cage, open the cage, *hic est*, hey presto —

J.J.: I don't want to hear —

LOWRIE: Who's Father Macnee?
J.J.: Magee —
LOWRIE: Magee, Macnee, who is he — ?
J.J.: A priest —
DENNIS: This must stop —
LOWRIE: *Allahu Akbar* —
J.J.: No, no. That was later, later —
LOWRIE: Hey presto —
J.J.: No, no —
LOWRIE: *Ce n'est pas nécessaire* —
J.J.: [*involuntarily*] *Il est mort* —
LOWRIE: *Hic est* —
J.J.: *Hoc est* —
LOWRIE: Hey presto —
J.J.: We have blood —
LOWRIE: Charlatan —
J.J.: Abracadabra —
LOWRIE: He wants a priest —
J.J.: I'll come, I'll come —
LOWRIE: Tell us, Mr Farr —
J.J.: [*a cry*] What would *you* have done?
LOWRIE: About what? About whom?
J.J.: About Father Magee.
LOWRIE: Tell us about Father Magee —
J.J.: He wants a priest —
LOWRIE: Who wants a priest — ?
J.J.: No, no no, *once* a priest —
LOWRIE: Did you say wants a priest or once a priest?
J.J.: Dennis, Dennis —
          [DENNIS *goes to him.*]
          – once a priest —
DENNIS: Yes, yes, I know —
LOWRIE: Once a priest, he said once a priest —
DENNIS: Let me take you to your room —
LOWRIE: Were you called on to act as a priest? Is that it, is that it — ?
          Were you called on to act as a priest?
J.J.: Yes, yes, yes, I left the cage — and was a priest again — a
          priest — [*turning on* LOWRIE] What would you have done?
          [*He weeps, all defences gone; sobbing*] What would you have
          done?

AUSTIN: [*after a moment; distressed*] Yes, weep. J.J., weep for all of us
here. What would we have done? It could happen to any of
us. The nightmare. To be called on. How would we have
answered? How would you have answered, Mr Lowrie, once
a priest?

LOWRIE: I'd have stayed in the cage. That's what Mr Farr should have
done. Stayed in the cage. Where he belongs.
[*He goes.*]

ANDY: At least our Mr Lowrie's not a hypocrite.
[J.J. *weeps.*]
[*Lights fade to blackout.*]

END OF ACT ONE

ACT TWO

SCENE ONE: Two days later. Dusk.

In the courtyard, DENNIS, ANDY, OLIVER *and* AUSTIN *are grouped around* J.J. *in silence. They are waiting. Then* LOWRIE *emerges from the house.* DENNIS *indicates somewhere for him to sit, but he prefers to be apart from the others, and hardly looks at* J.J.
When they are settled:

J.J.: A Sunday, the eighteenth of our captivity. The hundred and thirtieth day. In the eye of the sun, the heat of a blowtorch. Father Magee appears. Emaciated and threadbare. Like his vestments. This was after my punishment. After they branded the cross on my back for shouting abuse during Mass. But I will keep up my derision, mumbling my insults, eyes closed. They think I'm praying now. 'Charlatan, abracadabra, *hic est, hoc est,* hey presto, we have blood.' Here's the scene. Blinding heat. Prison yard. Five of us in a cage. A hooded guard, armed, high on hash, dangerous. Enter the priest. *Et introibo ad altare Dei.* He carries a tin mug and an enamel plate he uses as chalice and paten. Only one of our number asks to be let out that day. My cell-mate, Jimmy Martin. Out he goes, kneels before Magee. From me, a constant mumbled commentary. 'Get it right, Father, strike your breast, *Domine, non sum dignus,* what, no bells?' And so on and so forth. Quietly, cowardly, until whatever he was using for wine and bread are placed under the magic spell. The priest crosses himself with the tin mug. *Sanguis Domini Nostri.* At this precise moment, he collapses, struggling not to spill the contents of his makeshift chalice. Somehow, Jimmy manages to get hold of it as the priest falls. The guard sniggers. Jimmy places the mug on the priest's chest and leans close to hear him. Minutes pass. Then, Jimmy hurries to the cage. Someone asks, 'Is he dead?' 'No,' Jimmy says, 'but near. His mind's wandering.' 'Listen,' says Jimmy, 'I'm going to say something now, something he's asked me to say. I'm just going to say it because it's what he asked. He wants a priest. I told him there wasn't one here. He was the only

priest. But he said to say, "Once a priest, always a priest,"
and one of you would come.' 'So. I'm going to say it,' says
Jimmy. '"Once a priest, always a priest."' And so from me:
'All right. I'll come.' I call to the guard, *'Mon frère, ouvrez la
porte. Je veux aider le prêtre.'* He lets me out. He sniggers
again. I go to Father Liam Magee, who lies dying in the
prison yard. 'Thank you,' he says, 'I knew you'd come. Hear
my confession.' I say, 'You've nothing to confess, you're a
good man.' But he begs me. I take his worn, grease-stained
stole and put it round my neck. I do what's required of me.
When I come to give him the sacrament I find the chalice
empty. The contents must have spilled in his fall. He
reaches under his cassock, into his soiled underpants and
produces a small phial of yellowish liquid. 'Please, please,'
he says. I take the phial and empty the contents into the tin
mug. He hands me his missal. I consecrate the yellow liquid
and, as I finish, the priest dies. Jimmy, witness to all this,
asks the question, 'What do we do with the consecrated
wine?' 'It's urine,' I say. 'It's white wine,' he says, 'and you
consecrated it.' I say, 'If you believe it's now blood, drink it.'
I turn to the guard. *'Le prêtre est mort.'* The guard laughs
crookedly, then raises his gun, takes aim at the priest's body
and fires. The shot goes wild. Jimmy says, 'He's trying to hit
the chalice.' So, I call to the guard, *'Ce n'est pas nécessaire. Il
est mort. Je veux rentrer dans la cage.'* But he fires again in the
direction of the corpse. And then, coolly, detached, ice in a
blast-furnace, I walk back to the body, take the mug and
gulp the contents. The guard cracks me with the back of his
hand across my face. I bleed from the nose and taste my own
blood. He puts Jimmy and me back in the cage and locks us
in. He fires a couple of shots into the priest's corpse. From
somewhere far off, the muezzin begins calling the faithful to
prayer: *'Allahu Akbar, Allahu Akbar.'* God is greater. There is
no God but God.

[*Silence.*]

ANDY: I would have done what you did, J.J.

OLIVER: Yes, yes, I suppose so, perhaps I would. I don't know, I don't
know.

AUSTIN: There was no choice.

LOWRIE: What about the Warden?

DENNIS: [*smiles*] You know me. Anything to oblige.

LOWRIE: You all belong in small rooms with rubber walls.

AUSTIN: With rubber what?

LOWRIE: Walls, walls, padded cells —

ANDY: Why?

LOWRIE: What you've described, Mr Farr, this so-called rediscovery of faith and priesthood is, well, the word that springs most trippingly to the tongue, is 'grotesque'.

DENNIS: Take no notice, J.J., he does it to provoke.

LOWRIE: Still protecting him, are you, Warden? Still afraid I might damage your penitent, I mean, patient?

J.J.: Why do you talk about me as if I weren't here?

LOWRIE: It goes deep, the withdrawal, the fantasy. I know very well where you are, and I'll fight you on your own ground.

DENNIS: Don't rise, J.J. It's a game.

LOWRIE: Yes, yes, all right, a game, let's play a game.

OLIVER: Must we turn everything into a game? Serious issues have been raised. Oh, don't let's turn it into a game.

AUSTIN: The English turn everything into a game. Their excuse is that anything enjoyable is more salutary than anything salutary. It's absurd, of course, but then it's English. It's the pride they take in their lumpy scepticism.

LOWRIE: Aren't you English?

AUSTIN: I? Of course. My scepticism is lumpier than most.

J.J.: [*to* LOWRIE] I'll play your game.
[*He covers his eyes with one hand.*]

LOWRIE: Calling for reinforcements? Bringing up the big guns? Asking for guidance from GHQ?
[J.J. *looks at him.*]
Right. [*to* AUSTIN] Mr — I'm sorry. I don't remember your name —

AUSTIN: Purvis —

LOWRIE: What is the opening sentence of *Seeing, Not Believing* by J.J. Farr?

AUSTIN: 'In the dying years of the present century, no reasonable person can be reasonable and religious.'

LOWRIE: [*to* J.J.] Your words.

J.J.: Yes.

LOWRIE: Are we then to understand that you are now no longer a reasonable person?

[*Groans from the others.*]

ANDY: Unfair. That was written ages ago. He's somebody else now.

AUSTIN: Quite. You have to forgive him, Mr — You see, J.J.'s an intellectual. He's allowed to change his mind.

J.J.: Until the eighteenth Sunday of my captivity, I'd never before had a direct experience of — [*He can't find the words.*] Neither as layman nor as priest. I followed a course expected of me. But on that Sunday, in the prison yard, I faced — I met — [*He falters.*]

LOWRIE: Go on, say it: 'God'.

J.J.: God, then.

[*The light is fading fast now.*]

LOWRIE: You say you met God. And you want me to take your word for that. Well, there's a difficulty here. Because for some curious reason your god doesn't allow all his creatures to meet him. So, I'm afraid, Mr Farr, you're going to have to prove him more conclusively. Prove this god who revealed himself to you, then we may be able to accept your experience of him. Prove your creator of space and time, existing beyond both.

[*Again the others groan.*]

DENNIS: Come Mr Lowrie, you have to do better than this. You're dealing with old pros here. We all know there's no satisfactory proof of God. If it were otherwise, we none of us would be in this house. We would still be priests.

LOWRIE: Right. And, as it's impossible to prove He exists, it's also impossible to accept any experience of Him. Therefore, He does not exist —

OLIVER: May not exist, surely, may not, there's the hell of it, may not —

LOWRIE: All right, may not exist and, therefore, any experience of something that may or may not exist, may or may not be a lump of shit.

ANDY: Disprove God.

OLIVER: Good, good, Andy, that's my point. That's impossible too, isn't it, Mr Lowrie? There's doubt for you —

LOWRIE: [*quite unruffled*] All right. Proof or no proof, surely Mr Farr's beliefs ought still to be reasonable. Because if they're unreasonable, they're total gibberish. We can test it. Let's test your creed, Mr Farr. You would now say, presumably, that you believe in one god who may or may not exist, the maker of heaven and earth — just consider these words — the maker of heaven and earth and of all things visible *and* invisible. The maker of invisible things? It's gibberish. You may as well say you believe in haberlacky domotribble trans-combasculation.

AUSTIN: I couldn't follow that —

DENNIS: You weren't meant to —

LOWRIE: Gibberish, mumbo-jumbo. Like your story, Mr Farr. These words. Cage. Was there a cage? Or are you describing an inner state? Priest. Was there a priest? Or were you project-ing a fantasy of your own past? Tin chalice, the eye of the sun, *Allahu Akbar*, the grease-stained stole, *le prêtre est mort*. Jumbled fragments of mounting hysteria. I'll tell you what happened during your captivity. You grew fearful of death, of eternal nothingness. You were terrified of dying.

ANDY: Not true. You said you'd test his creed but you stopped short. 'I believe in the Resurrection of the Dead and the Life of the World to come.'

LOWRIE: Resurrection? What's that if it isn't an opiate to counter the fear of death? Death shall be conquered, *etcetera, etcetera.* Why should death need to be conquered if it isn't fearful? Why not just let it be?

ANDY: [*edgy*] He's secure. You are floundering.

[*J.J. has been, and is, alert during all this. The arguments buzz round him, over him, through him.*]

LOWRIE: Secure in what? In the life hereafter? Do you honestly believe that in the dying years of the present century it's possible for a reasonable being to believe in a life after death? Take a sampling, any section of the population you like, at random. Walk into any university and ask, 'Do you believe in life after death?' Ask surgeons gathered around the operating table, looking into the blood and mess of human beings. 'Do you believe that if your patient dies he or she will enjoy a life hereafter?' Ask lawyers, teachers, men of business, artists. Ask a biologist if he has evidence of life beyond the grave. Stop people in the street and you know very well what their answer will be. We all know, the rational side of us knows, what the answer must be.

OLIVER: That's very naughty of you, Mr Lowrie. When I was being

trained that's what my moral tutor would have called 'gross
generalisation'. Surely there will be individuals, doctors,
lawyers —

ANDY: Sociologists —

OLIVER: Yes, even sociologists, scientists and, most obvious of all,
people in the street. Individuals, Mr Lowrie, who will say
they expect life after death.

LOWRIE: The most extreme form of wishful thinking known to the
human animal. Lip-service, historical excreta heaped on us,
generation after generation, humbug and hypocrisy, endless,
untreated shit.

     [Darkness.]

AUSTIN: I should like to say something. Will you, Mr Lowrie, permit
an old man to ask why you, who make so much of reason,
should argue so unreasonably?

DENNIS: It's his game, Austin —

AUSTIN: Game or not, it's very disagreeable. Weren't you ever taught
at school or university or at your seminary that argument is
best when devoid of abuse? Argument in a civilised world
must be polite, reasoned and rational, otherwise chaos re-
sults.

LOWRIE: Yes, yes, yes, in your old-fashioned, ideal, embroidered
world, yes. But these things matter to me. It's all that matters
to me. The unmasking of the lies.

AUSTIN: Stop lecturing and hectoring —

     *[DENNIS turns up the light over the door to the house, and
to J.J.'s room.]*

LOWRIE: And do you know what breeds the lies? Fear, fear of death.
That's what Mr Farr experienced, and that's what holds him
hostage, nothing else.

ANDY: Is that what being alive feels like to you? Like a hostage taken
at random? Is that how existence seems to you? Violent,
cruel, without reason? Is that how you've come to view your
own life?

LOWRIE: Don't turn this on me, it's him we're talking about.

ANDY: I begin to see. To you life corresponds exactly to his experience in that prison, in that cage. Meaningless, an animal
existence, devoid of purpose and spirit.

LOWRIE: Any other interpretation in the dying years of the present

century and in the light of modern scientific knowledge
would be fanciful.

DENNIS: Science, science, the new religion, the old religion. You
allow scientists to ask, 'How did this or that come about?
Why does this or that occur?' After all, science itself thrives
on the questions 'how' and 'why'. Only when J.J. — and
others — ask, 'How does it come about that we exist or why
should we be here at all?' only then do you say, 'There is no
answer.' In every other aspect of life we search for reasons
why things occur, so to ask the ultimate questions about
existence is nothing more than the most logical, reasonable
thing we could do. Aristotle said we look for reasons why
things exist because they are not self-explanatory. He said
that everything in motion must be moved by something else,
that everything in the world is motivated by some inner
energy to become something greater than it is. Going back-
wards, man grows out of the child, the child from the
embryo, the embryo from the ovum, and so on, and so on,
and so on, until what? *Primum mobile immotum,* a prime
mover unmoved, incorporeal, indivisible, spaceless, sexless,
passionless, changeless, perfect, eternal. God. Science en-
courages us to seek ultimate explanations which, incidental-
ly, it is itself unable to provide. You allow it in science, but
not, as it were, in life. [*smiles*] I take no view, you understand,
I simply make the point.

LOWRIE: But why should there be an ultimate explanation of the
universe? Why should we assume anything at all? Science
obliterates Aristotle. Facts, verifiable facts, that's what I'm
interested in. These are the facts: the world has no purpose,
no inherent spiritual power, no beauty, no morality, no
rationale. Those are all interpretation. We are cogs in a
mechanical process. Facts. The universe is a result of accident. There is no ultimate explanation. No one has, or had,
or ever will have, immortality. Nature is purposeless. Facts.
We live, we endure, we die.

OLIVER: But that's also a set of beliefs, isn't it? Weren't we taught
that? I do believe we were. You can't prove your set of beliefs
either.

DENNIS: You want facts and logic and reason. Faith, absolute faith in

a creator, with all its spiritual implications, is not something
that needs to be proved or disproved. Surely they taught you
that in your seminary. That's what they taught me. Faith is
something beyond dispute. You either have it or you don't.
Faith is. Or is not.

AUSTIN: That's very good, Dennis. No help whatsoever, but very
good.

OLIVER: And what about the poor people who took J.J. hostage?
There's no point in saying to the terrorists, prove your faith.
They have faith and believe it to be the only faith, their cause
the only cause. That's a question of their belief, isn't it, a
matter of fact, not open to argument? In Dennis's sense,
their faith is beyond dispute. Am I right? Andy, am I right?

ANDY: But that's Mr Lowrie's position, too. I said you saw your life
as hostage to misfortune but I was wrong. You are at the
other end of the telescope. You're not the hostage, you're
the terrorist. The man with the gun who imprisons all
opposing thought in a damp, crowded cell. You believe your
interpretation is the only interpretation. But if it's facts
you're after, Mr Lowrie, then you had better come to terms
with the fact of J.J.'s experience —

LOWRIE: His experience is a series of random events initiated by
madmen which in turn made him mad. A mosaic of which he
remembers only the most striking shapes and the most
glaring colours. The prison cell, the tunnel that leads to the
Roman arena, the branding of a cross on his back, the priest
dying in his arms. The shapes and colours not of faith but of
fear. And 'All faith in the supernatural is a neurotic device to
deaden the fear of death.'

ANDY: You're deaf, you don't hear him, it wasn't any of those
things, certainly not the dying priest or the torture or the
pain. It wasn't fear of his own death —

LOWRIE: What, then?

J.J.: It was taking God, or piss, into my mouth.

[*Silence.*]

[*Exasperated,* LOWRIE *suddenly storms back into the
house.*]

AUSTIN: Anyone else being bitten to death?

[*He exits.*]

OLIVER: Time for bed.

[*He exits.*]

DENNIS: I think we could have done without that, J.J.

[*He exits.*]

[J.J. *covers his face with his hands.*]

[*Slowly, deliberately,* ANDY *places a chair at the odd angle, sideways on to* J.J. ANDY *sits. He doesn't face* J.J. *but* J.J. *faces him.*]

[*Silence.*]

[ANDY *quietly hums 'Three Old Ladies'.* J.J. *lowers his hands.* ANDY *smiles.*]

ANDY: I'm here, J.J. I won't look at you. I won't say a word.

J.J.: [*searching*] Yes, word, word, words. Words won't stretch. Words fall short — go so far and disintegrate. Before the word, before the beginning, there has to be a death, I think, then sleep, and the — dream, and the waking — inside the dream — even birth is not the word. It's a kind of coming into being, isn't it, a kind of intuition of being? Here, then, now, there. I want to use the word union, but that's misleading. There was a union certainly, no doubt of that, I and — this — this — No, no, not light, but light of a sort — two selves — one so low as to be worthless, but knowing itself to be the other — higher — nameless —

[ANDY *slowly turns to look at him.*]

Simply. This may be something. Peacefulness because there was no connection with time. The terrorists worship time, the past and the future and so they persecute and make wars. It's dark but radiantly clear. There is no — separateness of anything — it's beyond understanding. I was able to hear the softest sounds loudly, see a distant point as though to touch it. And it was *in* me. In me. In my mouth, my gullet, my intestine, my bowels. And there were beautiful things, too. The making of beds and the cleaning of the cell and eating the dry, glutinous rice. It didn't matter what happened to me then. I was free. And it was in me. Outside me. Nameless.

[*Silence.*]

[ANDY *rises quickly.*]

ANDY: [*hurrying away*] And I'll be late for work —

[*And as he goes:*]

[*Lights fade to blackout.*]

SCENE TWO: Later that evening. 10 p.m.

In his room, J.J. *is eating from a tray: a simple meal of yoghurt and an orange. His concentration on each mouthful is absolute.*

In the courtyard, a stab of torchlight as DENNIS *enters from around the side of the house.*

As DENNIS *turns,* LOWRIE *comes out of the house. He carries a carrier bag with something in it. He is crossing towards* J.J.'s *room when he sees* DENNIS. *He hides the carrier bag behind his back and stops.*

DENNIS: Taking the air, Mr Lowrie?

LOWRIE: [*slight hesitation*] No — I — I thought I left a book out here — I'm working — I need —

DENNIS: I don't know how you can work in this weather. Clammy, like Rome in midsummer.

LOWRIE: Rain's forecast.

        [He goes back into the house.]

DENNIS: Is it?

        [He goes to J.J.'s *door, knocks once and opens it.]*

        Sorry to disturb you, J.J., but you won't forget to lock this door, will you?

        *[*J.J. *is barely aware of him. He continues to eat.]*

        *[*DENNIS *checks the windows. As he does so there is a knock on* J.J.'s *inner door.]*

J.J.: Yes?

        *[*LOWRIE, *with the carrier bag hidden behind his back, enters* J.J.'s *room.]*

LOWRIE: I'd like to see you, but if it's not convenient —

J.J.: Sit. I won't be a moment.

        *[*J.J. *finishes eating.* LOWRIE *surreptitiously places the carrier bag near the foot of the bed so that* J.J. *can't see it.]*

        *[*DENNIS *exits, going on his rounds.]*

        [When J.J. *finishes, he turns to* LOWRIE *and gazes at him.* LOWRIE *becomes uncomfortable.]*

LOWRIE: I've come to apologise.

J.J.: No need.

        *[*LOWRIE *laughs nervously.]*

        [Pause.]

[LOWRIE*'s manner is now, for the most part, conciliatory: he is up to something.*]

LOWRIE: [*a sort of smile*] I can't explain why I become so obnoxious. It's a kind of showing-off. I think it's because I need to demonstrate my sincerity. Adolescent, really. I'm sorry.

J.J.: Nothing wrong with that.
[*He smiles.*]

LOWRIE: I need to demonstrate my absolute freedom from faith. You see, my priesthood became fraudulent.

J.J.: Tell me.

LOWRIE: Basic stuff. Instead of feet, I saw hooves. Instead of hands, claws. People, a herd. Music, an algebraic formula, poetry, the accident of alphabet. And all the glory of the world a misunderstanding by a self-regarding species. [*smiles*] The animal kingdom. Not uncommon, I believe.

J.J.: Was it sudden — ?

LOWRIE: Not sudden, no, intermittent. Nightmares at first. Then, in waking hours, mental skirmishes, raids on my consciousness. For example, when I tried to pray. Or during Mass. Then, more and more frequently. Until it was unbearable.

J.J.: What did you do?

LOWRIE: I cut my wrists. [*He shows the scars; again the smile.*] You see, I know all about cries for help.

J.J.: And were your cries answered?

LOWRIE: Yes. By you, for one.

J.J.: Me?

LOWRIE: Your books. While I was recovering, I began to read you. When you dismantled God, you gave me the confidence I needed. That seemed to be important then, while I was still a priest. I was a convert, you see. I've always been a convert.

J.J.: But I left room for doubt.

LOWRIE: I didn't see that at the time.

J.J.: What did you do?

LOWRIE: I had to find a way of earning my living again. Most of all, I wanted to continue my studies. I'd read psychology before becoming a priest and needed to bring myself up to date. And then, I wanted to write a book. I found a publisher. He gave me a small advance. I studied and wrote by day. At night I worked in a bakery. It was a kind of nether world. I'd use the word purgatory in its true sense. The book was published. It was well reviewed —

J.J.: By me, you said —

LOWRIE: Yes, by you. Among others. Then my bishop asked to see me, to discuss my future. He advised me to take time to reflect on what I was doing. I resisted, of course, but then he suggested this house. 'A place to hang up your collar for a while,' he said. And when I learned that you lived here, I decided it was where I wanted to be.

J.J.: You must be disappointed.

LOWRIE: It's also why I want to help you. I owe you a debt. You showed me the way to truth.

J.J.: But the ground's shifted, hasn't it? Hasn't it?

LOWRIE: I want to help you, Mr Farr —

J.J.: I know —

LOWRIE: [flaring] Don't mock me.

J.J.: I don't. Believe me. I know you have this need —

LOWRIE: You say — you say now — that you left room for doubt, a safety-net, a silver-plated agnosticism engraved with your initials. Give me the benefit then, of viewing your present state in exactly the same half-light. Allow yourself room for doubt now.

J.J.: I'll allow anything.
        [Pause.]

LOWRIE: I'm going to be blunt. You don't have to be a trained psychologist to know that what happened to you was a psychotic transference —

J.J.: You may well be right —

LOWRIE: — the moment of revelation, the comfort you gave a dying man —

J.J.: Yes, yes, odd thing, the psyche —

LOWRIE: That was the moment, wasn't it? The priest dying in your arms, and you became that priest? Shaman. Witch doctor. Tragic hero and intermediary.

J.J.: I think you've got the wrong man. These words, you see. Not sure about these words —

LOWRIE: No, no, listen to me. I don't deny that you were put through a savage, horrifying ordeal. As a result of this admittedly intense experience, in which you are obliged to revert to your priestly function, you now claim to have regained faith in a god in whom you once said it was impossible to believe. I am asking you to question the validity of your experience. In the face of irrational forces you ran for shelter. Now, when was your life most sheltered and most ordered? When were you most respected, unquestioned? In your priestly habit. What you describe is a classic pattern, a retreat into familiar territory, an escape to safety. All I ask is that you admit this possibility and seek treatment. What can you lose? At best it will save you pain, unhappiness and despair.

J.J.: Shall I tell you what it feels like? It's as though you insist on talking about someone who isn't here. But here I am. I know it's hard to grasp — I was there — now I'm here — being taken hostage, being branded, the communion — everything, had one meaning then — but not —

LOWRIE: Well, now, I was waiting for that word. Meaning. The god-tyrant directing our lives in ways too complex for us to comprehend. Was there also meaning for those who were taken out and shot?

J.J.: Yes, if you believe that death isn't an end. No, if you believe that death is the worst thing that can happen.

LOWRIE: I do believe that, that's precisely what I do believe.

J.J.: But what difference does death make?

LOWRIE: What?

J.J.: Fear of death may be your prison.

LOWRIE: Don't turn it on me. I know how the priestly mind works. You believe there was meaning in what happened to you. Don't you? Don't you? You think the whole bloody event was organised by your god to bring you back into priesthood. You think that the murder of three innocent men was simply part of some divine plan for the salvation of J.J. Farr.

J.J.: I don't know the meaning for them, I don't know the meaning for me —

LOWRIE: There was no meaning —

J.J.: You may well be right —

LOWRIE: — not for you, not for the dead. What was the purpose of their being taken out and shot? Are they now looking down on you, cheering you on, rejoicing in their martyrdom, is that what you believe — ?

[*Silence.*]

J.J.: The nights are drawing in.

LOWRIE: What?

J.J.: Can't you smell it? The slightest chill. The day's gone. Or going. The earth's a good stand-by. It's our one sure footing.

LOWRIE: You see? You avoid answering. You won't face what's happened. You're ill.

J.J.: [*vigorous; pointing at the orange on the tray*] Look — look — [*touches the orange*] touch — [*sniffs it*] smell — [*places the orange in* LOWRIE's *hand*] feel. How can I — ? What can I — ? [*He begins to remove his shirt.*] Take off the dressing. Go on, go on. Put your hand on the scar, don't say anything, just feel this cross —

[LOWRIE *doesn't move.* J.J. *manages to remove the dressing.* LOWRIE *gazes at the scar.*]

Feel it.

LOWRIE: But that's not a cross, it's a crescent moon.

[J.J. *looks at him in disbelief, twists and turns in an effort to see the scar, then goes into the bathroom. After a second, his laughter can be heard.*]

[LOWRIE *picks up the carrier bag and takes from it a bottle of wine and a corkscrew. He opens the wine.* J.J. *becomes aware of what he is doing.*]

[*calling to* J.J.] I'm going to help you whether you want to be helped or not.

[J.J. *returns.*]

God didn't mark you, terrorists marked you. The sign you were given was not the one you wanted. And when you say you took God into your mouth, you took urine.

J.J.: Urine, wine, sand, blood, God, stuff, of my own making —

LOWRIE: [*jumping on it*] Of your own making, precisely. Could it be of my making, then, since I, Kenneth Lowrie, duly ordained a Catholic priest, who saw faith as a sham, who tried to take his own life, who knows, as a rational human being, that there is no god, that there is no life after death, still have that same magical power as you have to transform wine into the blood of your Lord, Jesus Christ?

J.J.: Is it important?

LOWRIE: I know a believer when I see one.

[*From his back pocket* LOWRIE *takes a small missal and*

opens it. He places the bottle of wine on the table and proceeds to consecrate it.]

J.J.: What are you doing?

LOWRIE: Latin for you, I think, Father. [*reading from the missal*] *Simili modo postquam coenatum est* —

J.J.: Don't — don't — please — don't do that —

LOWRIE: [*continuous*] — *accipiens et hunc praeclarum Calicem in sanctas ac venerabiles* —

J.J.: Stop. Stop, for your own sake —
[*He seems about to go for* LOWRIE *but turns away.*]

LOWRIE: [*continuous*] — *manus suas: item tibi gratias agens, bene* —
[*He makes the sign of the cross over the bottle of wine.*]
— *dixit, deditque discipulis suis, dicens: Accipite, et bibite ex eo omnes. Hic est enim calix sanguinis mei, novi et aeterni testamenti: mysterium fidei: qui pro vobis et pro multis effundetur in remissionem peccatorum.*
[*He genuflects.*]
Haec quotiescumque feceritis, in mei memoriam facietis.
[*Silence.*]
Is that now the blood of Jesus Christ? If so, what shall we do with it?
[*He holds up the bottle.*]
[*Stillness.*]
[*Very deliberately, slowly,* J.J. *takes the bottle from* LOWRIE *and pours some of the wine on the carpet.* LOWRIE *recoils, shocked. Then* J.J. *begins to swig from the bottle.*]
[*involuntarily*] You've been eating, you should have made yourself sick.

J.J.: [*swigging*] I'll be sick, I'll be sick —
[J.J. *starts to sway, continuing to drink. He finishes the bottle.*]

LOWRIE: There's some on the floor, you spilled some on the floor —
[J.J. *drops to his knees and starts to lick the floor.*]
[*barely audible*] You're insane — look, look at you, you're licking wine stains from a carpet — stop it, stop it —

J.J.: [*almost unable to rise*] Oh my God —

LOWRIE: There was no intention — it can't be valid — how can it be anything but wine?
[J.J. *tries to stand.*]

J.J.: Did you say, was there — did you — *in vaetam aeternam* — *Amen, amen,* let me see your hands — let me — you're not a priest, you're an alchemist —

> [*He lunges clumsily towards* LOWRIE.]

LOWRIE: Don't touch me —

J.J.: — and you're not the first. A bishop told me that once, while paddling at Blackpool, he held out his hands over the waves and consecrated the Irish Sea. And this madman now believes whenever it rains the earth is being drenched in God's blood. But every millimetre of sea and land, every leaf and pebble was consecrated long before that, before him, before you, before me, before let there be light. You think it needs you to do it, but it doesn't, it's been done. So let's drink to that, let's drink this wine, let's have a party, let's be drunk —

LOWRIE: You need treatment —

J.J.: [*overlapping*] — the heat —

> [*He makes for the door and staggers out into the courtyard.* LOWRIE *comes to the door and watches him gasping for breath.*]

The world is spinning — I am — I — am — extremely — I have — [*triumphant*] I have seen a new heaven and a new earth — [*shouting*] *Hic est* — *hoc est* — *Allahu Akbar* —

> [*He falls to the ground.*]

[*shouting*] Charlatan. [*then, quietly*] I see three of you. [*laughs*] Don't tell the Warden —

> [LOWRIE *goes.*]

> [J.J. *sits grinning.*]

Good old Jimmy Martin. I remember the naughty verses —
  'The first lady's name was Elizabeth Porter,
  She was the Bishop of Chichester's daughter,
  There on account of some overdue water,
  Brought on by a half-pint of beer.'

> [*A spill of light from the house.*]

  'The second lady's name was Dorothy Humphrey,
  She sat down but then could not get her bum free,
  She said, "Never mind, for I'm perfectly comfy,
  Nobody knows that I'm here."'

> [DENNIS, *tying the cord of his dressing-gown, comes out from the house and goes to* J.J. *He draws back at the smell of wine on* J.J.*'s breath.*]

'The third lady's name was Virginia Wender,
There on account of a stocking suspender,
Caught in the hair of her feminine gender,
A terribly painful affair.'
[*near to passing out*] A terribly painful affair —
      [*He falls back, moans, and begins to retch violently.*
      DENNIS *goes to him.*]
      [*Lights fade to blackout.*]

SCENE THREE: *Eight hours later. Just before 7 a.m.*

In his room, J.J. *is asleep in bed.*

In the courtyard, LOWRIE *stands, eyes closed, still as a statue. After a little time he opens his eyes and breathes rhythmically as if summoning strength — a preparation for something. Slowly he looks around, at the house, at the sky. Then from his pocket he takes an envelope. He goes to the door of* J.J.'s *room and slips the envelope under the door.*

J.J. *sleeps.*

ANDY *enters from inside the house in a state of some agitation.*

ANDY: J.J., J.J. — [*sees* LOWRIE] Mr Lowrie, I've got to talk to someone —

LOWRIE: Not now — I don't want — I can't — not now —

ANDY: [*overlapping*] I'd have woken Dennis, but you'll do, you'll do —

LOWRIE: [*overlapping*] You're supposed to be at work —

ANDY: [*overlapping*] This business has upset me —

LOWRIE: Why are you back from work?

ANDY: I didn't get to work —

LOWRIE: I have something I must do —

ANDY: [*grabbing hold of* LOWRIE] I've got to talk to you —

LOWRIE: I can't — this is not the time — let go of me —

ANDY: Listen to me —

LOWRIE: You'll wake the house.

ANDY: Listen to me —

LOWRIE: I don't want to listen to you —

ANDY: Bastard, bastard, you and Farr, you're both bastards, you

masturbate thoughts and feelings like cheap whores in a
massage parlour, it's upset me, it's upset me, it's upset the
whole house —

LOWRIE: Let go — let go —

ANDY: I don't think she could have been more than seventeen —

LOWRIE: What — ?

ANDY: [*holding onto* LOWRIE's *arm with both hands*] Please listen, but
don't look at me, turn away, don't look at me —

LOWRIE: [*anguish increasing*] Please, let go, please, please — I won't be
here much longer —

ANDY: [*overlapping*] You and Farr, wine, blood, Jesus, we've got
lives to lead, lives to lead, I've been such a good boy for so
long — what's faith and God and — just listen — just listen.
Don't look at me.

> [*Pause. He lets go of* LOWRIE, *who manages to slip away
> unnoticed.*]

She was young. Old routine. Used to do it even when —
[*Pause.*] Tonight. Revivalist meeting. Sat at the back.
Drunks, druggies, derelicts, me. She came round with the
collection. No make-up, rosy cheeks, damp eyes, spotlessly
clean fingernails cut short. I put a fiver in the box. Afterwards, I followed her. She walked quickly, humming a
hymn. So, I hummed it, too. She looked around. She remembered me. She remembered the fiver in the box. Old
trick. Got talking. Talked of revelation, redemption, I know
the game, got her going, it always does, God is love, I said.
She began to pant. Held her hand. Down the alley, God is
love. Relax, relax, I said. And before you could say
Armageddon we were at it like Seventh Day Adventists.
Then at the moment of ecstasy, she cried, 'Hallelujah!' and
that's the best compliment I've had from any girl. It's all
right, isn't it, Mr Lowrie, no harm done, it's all right?

> [J.J. *rises and puts on his dressing-gown. He discovers the
> envelope near the door.*]

No it isn't, is it? No. Wish I could break the umbilical. Know
I'm going to be punished, know it. The fire, the bloody fire
— Say it's all right. What's it cost you?

> [ANDY *turns and realises that* LOWRIE *is not there.*]

> [J.J. *comes out into the courtyard.*]

J.J.: Where's Mr Lowrie?

ANDY: He was here a moment ago.

J.J.: Find him.

[ANDY *starts to go but stops dead.*]

ANDY: [*seeing* LOWRIE *offstage*] Oh hell, no, no —

[LOWRIE *enters bleeding, having cut his wrists. He staggers, then stumbles, and is unable to rise.*]

[ANDY *does not move.*]

J.J.: [*severe*] Get Dennis.

[ANDY *goes.*]

[J.J. *fetches a cloth or towel from his room. He returns to* LOWRIE *and attends to him.*]

LOWRIE: Leave me alone — don't come near me —

J.J.: [*tough*] Lie still —

[J.J. *applies tourniquets above* LOWRIE's *elbows.*]

[*while applying the tourniquets*] You stupid sod. In all the months of captivity, no one, not one single hostage, when the bluntest, rustiest, dirtiest razor might have seemed like salvation, not once did anyone whisper the possibility of suicide. What do you want me to feel? Sympathy? Alarm? Responsibility?

[LOWRIE *whimpers.*]

Shall I tell you what I really feel? Disgust. So easy, isn't it, so privileged, just take your own life, put an end to it, duck out, just look at you, look at you —

[DENNIS, *tying the cord round his dressing-gown, comes from the house, followed by* ANDY, *who hovers in the background.*]

DENNIS: Is he all right?

J.J.: Yes, of course he's all right.

[OLIVER, *also in a dressing-gown, appears.*]

OLIVER: What's happened, is Mr Lowrie hurt?

J.J.: [*to* OLIVER] Make tea, hot and sweet.

[OLIVER *exits.*]

ANDY: Will he be all right?

J.J.: Shock, that's all, he's lost some blood, but not serious, not at all serious —

ANDY: [*helping* J.J.] Why, Mr Lowrie, why?

DENNIS: Not now, Andy, not now —

ANDY: Why should he do this to us? I thought he was beginning to like it here —

DENNIS: Leave him be, Andy.

J.J.: I'll tell you why. Because he's like all of you here, Andy. You don't live in this world, you never have. Too much thought, not enough heart. You, Lowrie, all of you. I wish I could feel sorry for all of you, but the problem is you all get on my bazonkers.

[ANDY *hovers.*]

ANDY: Should we get a doctor?

J.J.: Andy, stop standing around like a spare prick at a wedding. Find some disinfectant, towels, bandages, go on —

[ANDY *goes, passing* OLIVER, *who returns with tea. He kneels beside* LOWRIE *and helps him to drink.*]

OLIVER: Mind, it's very hot. Slowly, slowly. [*to* J.J.] What a dreadful thing. I've brought a couple of my tranquillisers. They're rather strong. Do you think it a good idea?

J.J.: Yes, yes, why not, yes, yes.

DENNIS: I'll telephone the doctor —

[*He exits.*]

OLIVER: [*quietly, to* LOWRIE] I am very sorry you were driven to such despair. Perhaps when you feel stronger you might want to have a little chat with me. I'm rather a woolly person, punctured by doubt. But I may be able to give comfort, who knows?

[ANDY *returns with a tray on which there is a bowl, cotton wool and a bandage. He puts them down beside* J.J.]

[*feeding* LOWRIE *the tea*] That's the way. [*giving him the tranquillisers*] Just put these on your tongue and down they go. I made the tea very sweet, very sweet indeed. Swallow. Swallow.

J.J.: [*to* LOWRIE] I'm putting on disinfectant. It'll remind you of incense. It may sting.

OLIVER: [*to* LOWRIE] There, good boy, all gone. You'll feel better. Bless you.

[DENNIS *returns.*]

[OLIVER *rises and* DENNIS *takes his place beside* LOWRIE.]

DENNIS: Do you want me to let anyone know what's happened? Do you want to see anyone? Your parents?

[*No response.*]

Have you brothers and sisters? A friend, perhaps?
[LOWRIE *tries not to cry.*]
We'll look after you. I think you'll agree we're equipped to do that, and when you feel better —
[AUSTIN *enters, dressed, carrying his canvas bag.*]

AUSTIN: Where is this rain we've heard so much about? On television a moment ago they talked about water rationing. And then they showed pictures of famine. Why do they always show pictures of famine at meal times?

OLIVER: Guilt, old chap, guilt.

AUSTIN: Ah, that rings a bell. [*seeing* LOWRIE] What's the matter with Mr Lowrie? Has he taken to sleeping out of doors?
[OLIVER *takes* AUSTIN *aside to explain, just as* LOWRIE *suddenly erupts, trying to tear off his bandages. All, except* J.J. *and* AUSTIN, *rush to attend to him and then* DENNIS *turns on* J.J.]

DENNIS: [*sudden, deeply-felt anger*] I lay this at your door, J.J. You've burst in, shattered our peace, and brought nothing but turmoil. I don't know where you are, J.J, in some rarefied turret. When do you ever talk about pain and misery and joy and despair and pleasure and beauty and love and the terrible glory of just being? In this house we are moderate men or we are nothing. Mr Lowrie's right. You don't belong here any more. You can't go on living here. I shall speak to the trustees. No, no, no, I'm sorry, I'm sorry, I'm sorry. It was hasty of me. Forget I said it, we'll talk about it, there's no need to do anything now —
[J.J. *goes quickly into his room, then quickly into his bathroom, out of sight.*]
[*Silence.*]

ANDY: I'll walk. I'll keep awake. I'll walk.

OLIVER: Should you? Shouldn't we all be together, for Dennis's sake? Moral support, that sort of thing —

ANDY: [*flaring*] All right, I'll stay, I won't walk. Now, now, now.
[*Silence.*]

DENNIS: It'll all be over soon. And so will the day and the night and the struggle for sleep. [*Pause.*] Did I say terrible things to J.J.?

OLIVER: No, no, no, you were quite right.

AUSTIN: Oughtn't you to get Mr Lowrie indoors?

OLIVER: He's asleep.

AUSTIN: [*enjoying it all*] When was the last time we had to get rid of a resident?

[*He sits and works on some embroidery.*]

OLIVER: Poor old Francis Barnaby.

ANDY: So it was. A dear fellow. But in his case we were either blind or naive. When I cleared out his room, the empty bottles under his bed filled three sacks. And I never saw him pissed. [*Pause; to* DENNIS] Sorry it fell on you, old chap. Unpleasant thing to have to do. But quite right, quite right. This chap needs help. But not J.J. Never J.J.

DENNIS: Francis Barnaby. Yes. I remember. Autumn leaves gusting. A chill wind. A chill room. [*smiles*] Chill-dren.

[*Silence.*]

OLIVER: What a twelvemonth this has been. David dying and my prostate. Now this.

AUSTIN: The Greeks ordered things so much better. They had the ostracon.

ANDY: The what?

AUSTIN: The ostracon. A piece of pottery, a chard, a flake of lime-stone on which it was possible to write a name. That was in the golden age, in Athens, when everything was lovely. [*smiles*] Some say in mid-winter, others a month or two later, the assembly was asked whether or not it would hold an ostracism. If the answer was yes, at the next convenient meeting each citizen took the flake of limestone, the ostra-con, and wrote on it the name of a person he believed threatened the stability of the state. No specific charges were brought. A valid ostracism required six thousand votes. The man against whom these votes were cast had, within ten days, to leave the city for ten years.

ANDY: In this house, it seems, they have to leave at once. Well, I suppose, all of us here have been through it in another place, at another time. In my case, twice. I've always believed my name was inscribed on an ostracon the day I was born. That was the first time.

DENNIS: It's what the terrorists feel who took J.J. hostage. What the hostages felt, too, no doubt. What, perhaps, Mr Lowrie feels. They believe the gates of the city are locked against them, but the gates of the city are of their own making.

ANDY: I always thought we were wrong to get rid of Francis. He never endangered the state. And, funny, his breath never smelt.

[J.J. *returns to his room; he is dressed. He starts to pack.*]

AUSTIN: Does anyone know why our Mr Lowrie tried to take his own life?

[*Silence.*]

OLIVER: In my worst moments I never despaired. It's Mr Lowrie's one act of humanity since he's been here. Poor, dear man.

DENNIS: Some nights, after my fall from grace, after my wife died, I used to wake and think of suicide. In a mysterious way, I found it a powerful solace. Thoughts of suicide got me through many a bad night.

[*He smiles.*]

[*Silence.*]

AUSTIN: [*in his own world*] A profound loss of faith is not cause enough for despair. I remember this. A long time ago. At the time of my greatest anguish. Someone I loved told me that when I made the sign of the cross, ballerinas all over Europe turned green with envy. That cheered me up. Too ridiculous. And, after all, who knows, faith may return? I've always thought that would be a lovely thing. And life is such an absurd sorrow. If there were no world and one was told to imagine it, how impossible that would be.

ANDY: I'll give you all one crumb of comfort. If God is dead, as the philosophers say, then it follows that the devil must have died, too. And that's an enormous relief.

LOWRIE: [*barely audible*] I want to see Mr Farr.

OLIVER: What, Mr Lowrie?

LOWRIE: Warden —

[DENNIS *goes to him.*]

LOWRIE: I want to see Mr Farr.

DENNIS: It can wait, Mr Lowrie. Let's get you into bed —

LOWRIE: Ask him if he'll see me.

[*The others watch as* DENNIS *goes to* J.J.'s *door and knocks. No response. He knocks again and goes in.*]

DENNIS: Mr Lowrie wants to see you.

J.J.: [*a short sound*] Ah.

DENNIS: He tried to kill himself before, you know.

J.J.: Yes, I know.

DENNIS: Perhaps we shouldn't have admitted him.

J.J.: Who can say?

DENNIS: I'm sorry about my outburst —

J.J.: We both understand why it's impossible for me to go on living here, don't we?

DENNIS: Can't we talk it over? I didn't mean it — [*Pause.*] Though I admit, it would be particularly difficult for me, having you here. I envy you, J.J. I'd give anything to escape from this — this subsidised limbo. To stand on my own two feet again. What will you do now?

J.J.: Stand on my own two feet again.

DENNIS: Will you — will you ask to go back?

J.J.: I have no plans.
         [*He packs the orange in his suitcase.*]

DENNIS: I know a man, in Scotland, Archie Craig, takes in all sorts — even married priests. Would you like me to write to him?
         [*J.J., taking his case, goes into the courtyard. He puts down the case then goes to* LOWRIE'*s side.*]

J.J.: You wanted to see me.

LOWRIE: [*quietly*] Warden —
         [DENNIS *goes to him.*]
         — ask everyone to leave us, please —

ANDY: Good, I can sleep now —
         [*All go, except* DENNIS.]

DENNIS: [*to* J.J.] Can you cope?
         [*No response.*]
         Call us if —
         [*He follows the others.*]
         [*For the most part* LOWRIE *now speaks as if from a dream, the effect of the sedative.*]

LOWRIE: Turn away, don't look at me.
         [J.J. *does so.*]

J.J.: I'm not looking.

LOWRIE: You were god to me. But now I know you don't exist. And that's a relief. Do I make myself clear? Am I coherent? I've had to go through a lot to prove you don't exist. Now I can get some peace and peace is what I'm really after.

J.J.: What did you mean in your note — 'Both things are acts of defiance'?

LOWRIE: What did I mean? What did I mean? Yes, yes, yes. Both things. The wine and my own blood. When I consecrated the wine. When I cut my wrists. Both acts of defiance.

J.J.: Who were you defying? Me?

LOWRIE: Not only you.

J.J.: Who?

LOWRIE: Who do you think?

[*Silence.*]

Know there isn't one. Know neither of you exist. Know there's nothing. Know death is death. Certain of it. Death is death. But have to — have to test that certainty. Need proof. A need to go — to the edge. Faith was like that. Edge of faith, priesthood. Bleak world, mine. And yours. Don't say anything. Don't want arguments. Or comfort. Or help. Or forgiveness. Or creeds. Or salvation. Please, please, don't say you'll pray for me. Just want you to know that I, I acknowledge a need for treatment. Now, leave me in peace. I'm free of you.

[*Silence.*]

J.J.: You're not free of anything.

LOWRIE: Charlatan —

[J.J. *goes to* LOWRIE *and holds him.*]

J.J.: In a cage, an animal tortured by animals, I had this — I don't want to make too much of it — but this — this image: in the world, with all its terror and pain and horror, there are scales tipped in favour of harmony, beauty, love, goodness, all the things you affect to deny. You can't put your faith in facts and reason. There's no logic in it, is there? Without those scales, so precariously weighted, the world would have disintegrated a hundred million years ago. The balance of goodness is slight but it exists outside of us, not our making —

LOWRIE: You talk shit. Untreated shit.

[J.J. *lets go of him.*]

This world, this world, one truth, *Allahu Akbar*, one truth, one truth, *Domine, non sum dignus*, one truth, this world, one truth —

[J.J. *gets his suitcase.* LOWRIE *continues to mumble.*]

J.J.: [*calling*] You can come back. We're finished.

LOWRIE: [*continuing, but losing consciousness*] — this truth, this world, charlatan, *hic est, hoc est,* hey presto, we have blood, *il est mort,* this world, *Allahu Akbar,* one truth, this truth —

[*The others return,* DENNIS *leading.*]

J.J.: Look after him.

[J.J. *takes the orange out of the suitcase and leaves it behind. He exits.*]

LOWRIE: [*continuing*] — one world, one truth, now, hey presto, wants a priest, *ce n'est pas nécessaire,* this truth, this world, this now, this now, now world, this truth, now world, now truth, now, truth —

[*His words become sounds, like a murmured prayer, as the others gather round to lift him.*]

[*Lights fade to blackout.*]

THE END